Meditations in Color

**Eradicate Stress and Anxiety by
Integrating Mindfulness Practice with
Coloring Books for Adults**

Jason Brenizer

First Edition: April 2017
Printed in the United States of America
ISBN: 978-0-9968653-4-0

Digital Tales
512 W. MLK Jr. Blvd. #289
Austin, TX 78701
Digital-Tales.com

To David Lynch.

Table of Contents

Jason Brenizer

Introduction

GUIDELINES AND SIGNPOSTS

The act of coloring detailed patterns releases us from stress, worry, anxiety, and all the other external stuff that keeps us from experiencing happiness and fulfillment in the present moment. That's a powerful result for a simple action that's fun and expressive.

Here are some general guidelines to follow while you color away your stress and anxiety...

> *- Focus on the image you are about to color.*

> *- Visualize that scene or the shapes involved.*

> *- Notice the thoughts and emotions the scene evokes in you.*

> *- Remember to breathe in and out deeply and regularly.*

> *- This will help you consider color scheme and overall direction you want to move in.*

> *- It will ground you in the present moment and free you from external stress and worry.*

- And remember, the only wrong way to color is to not do it at all.

There is another benefit to consider if you are a parent. Imagine sitting side-by-side with your child, each of you coloring your own book, and maybe even sharing your pens or pencils. What an amazing way to deeply connect with your family, especially in the modern world where TV, computers, phones, and screens all vie for our attention and often cause feelings of isolation.

You can learn more about our range of coloring books for adults and other resources that help wash away stress and anxiety at **unlockmyzen.com.**

Not only will you discover inspiring images to color, you will also receive gentle lessons in gratitude, explorations into the teachers of past wisdom, insights on self-healing, and habits for happiness.

Part 1

Simple Actions Yield Big Benefits for Body, Mind, and Spirit

Chapter 1

Coloring Away Your Worries

THE ADULT COLORING BOOK CRAZE

It seems that the current craze of coloring books for grown-ups came out of nowhere. But the prescription for adults to color away their stresses and anxieties can be traced all the way back to Carl Jung, one of the founders of modern psychology.

Jung believed that coloring could help his patients access the mysteries of their subconscious and give them deeper self-knowledge.

So even if you picked up a coloring book for adults to simply pass the time and alleviate boredom, you will likely get the chance to uncover some long-forgotten experiences that continue to drive your reactions without you even knowing. That is a powerful tool built into something that is relaxing and fun.

TOOLS FOR SERENITY & HAPPINESS

You might be wondering, "What kind of coloring tools are best?"

According to ColoringBooks.net, adults should walk on by the box of crayons and make a b-line for the colored pencils or gel pens. When practicing tuning in to the present moment, precision is paramount.

That doesn't mean you need to get bent out of shape if you color out of the lines or accidentally color in a face a shade that you might be inclined to describe as "alien-green". Learning to let go of your inner criticisms is one of the major benefits of tying a physical activity to the practice of being aware of "the now".

If you hear that inner voice making a judgement, however reasonable it sounds, try to put this practice into perspective. Ask yourself this... "Am I performing heart surgery?"

4

THE BUZZING MIND

From time to time, many of us experience feelings of heightened worry, panic, and hyper-vigilance. Some of us swim in these states of being with an uncomfortable regularity. These emotional states have been shown to correlate with higher levels of activity in the part of the brain called the amygdala.

This is sometimes referred to as the reptilian brain. It's where the flight or fight response engages, and no amount of intellectual understanding of what's going on seems to help the situation.

The act of coloring can actually dial down that response in a big way.

Feelings of anger can recede. Intense bouts of worry can be soothed. If anyone has ever suggested that you suffer from Post-Traumatic Stress Disorder, or PTSD, the activity of putting pen or pencil to paper is an amazingly simple tool to give you much needed release and relief.

YOU AND YOUR INNER CHILD

Coloring can take us back to a simpler time. A time when we didn't have to worry about the mortgage or rent, the politics of the workplace, or troublesome world events.

We can all benefit from an activity that invokes the somewhat less complicated times of childhood.

The idea is to loosen your grip on the reins of your life, just a little bit. This will let us slip back to a time when we did not have so many responsibilities. More importantly, we get to rekindle the experience of doing something just because we want to, for the pure joy of it.

It's so easy to get caught up in doing things that matter or make a difference. But maintaining an iron grip of control quickly squeezes the joy out of life. Let your inner kid go out and play. It's okay if he or she stays out past dinnertime. Why not, just this once?

COLORING AND YOUR BRAIN

MY WHAT A BIG BRAIN YOU HAVE...

We have been talking a lot about the emotional benefits of coloring, but the practice has intellectual benefits as well. The two go hand in hand. Or rather hemisphere to hemisphere.

By utilizing areas of the brain that enhance focus, concentration, problem solving, and organizational skills, the fight or flight areas hold less dominion on our experience in the present moment. Coloring detailed pictures activates all those properties at once, and puts us into a kind of soothing trance. As you consider and implement complex color schemes and patterns, you will find anxiety and worry losing their hold on you.

A COUNTER-INTUITIVE SOLUTION...

Coloring engages both sides of your brain. Some sections of the brain fire up when we think about balance and subtle interplays of color and contrast. Other parts engage when we physically apply colored pencil or pen to paper. We are working on both problem solving and fine motor skills at the same time.

With all that going on right in front of you, in the here and now, thoughts about your day might still pop up from moment to moment, but they tend not to cling for too long. In repetitive, creative actions that have low stakes, we begin to feel more inner peace and happiness.

ART THERAPY VERSUS COLORING SOLO

As you tune in to your thoughts and feelings more and more, some wonderful revelations might surface. But some strange or troubling thoughts you had been blind to before could enter your awareness, too. This is great news! It means you are moving through the fog of denial.

When confronting some significant emotional issues, true art therapy led by a certified teacher can accelerate your grasp on happiness and emotional growth.

But that doesn't mean coloring solo should be jettisoned for the art therapy studio. We all learned as kids that you had to practice at home to truly integrate the lessons you learned at school. Knowing something intellectually and integrating it mentally and emotionally are two different layers of understanding.

The practice of coloring on a regular basis helps ease your mind, nurtures your inner child, and makes you feel restored. So even if you choose to attend art therapy, keep on coloring away at home or the coffee shop!

Part 2

Coloring and the Five Senses

Chapter 2

The Sense of Sight

IN THE BEGINNING

Before you begin to color, let's take a moment to key in to your tools. Take a look at your gel pens or colored pencils and ask yourself some simple questions.

Is the box new? Is it crisp and clean, or is it an old friend, full of character?

Look at the tips of your pencils. Are they all sharp or are some blunt? No level of sharpness is the wrong level. Maybe you prefer some of them snub-nosed because you can get a different coloring effect with them that way.

Look at the tips of some of your gel pens. Maybe they are clean and pristine. Or they could have smears of long-time use. Again, just notice how they are without making a judgement of right or wrong, good or bad.

Are the pencils the same height? Maybe some are taller than others? The short ones have been well-loved and might be your go-to colors.

The same goes for the height of the ink for gel pens. Take a moment to really look and see the differences.

THE LINES YOU DRAW

Notice whether the colored lines you are sketching onto the page are short or long. You will find over time that each technique has its uses.

If you begin to realize you always do it one way, why not try it another way? What's the worst that can happen? You color out of the lines? That's not a big thing. This is a coloring book, not the Sistine Chapel.

Are your strokes soft or heavy?

Vary the pressure of your pen or pencil on the page. See if you can make your marks feathery and light. Next, try filling in a section of the design dense and dark.

Do your lines all go in one direction? What about cross-hatching? Or swirls?

PERSPECTIVE

Look at one small section of the page. Really see the detail.

Are the lines of the design straight or curvy? Thick or thin?

Are your coloring marks tight and precise or are they broad and relaxed?

Don't worry about all the areas you haven't yet colored. There is no need to rush forward. You can take all the time in the world to color this particular image.

Alternatively, if you feel more relaxed by taking a looser approach, then by all means, color as fast as you like.

Ultimately, the act of coloring is the most powerful when you feel your worry wash away, and you learn to let go of the pressures of modern life. Letting go of a false sense of control paradoxically gives us freedom. And who doesn't want more freedom?

THE PERSPECTIVE OF DISTANCE

Step back and get a sense of the bigger picture

How do all your colors blend together?

Is there a lot of contrast? Or maybe you see a subtle shift in similar tones?

Either answer is right and good. There is no wrong. Just note what you see on the page without making any judgements about the results.

In life, as in coloring, you might find that the little mistakes mean very little when viewed at a distance.

EMOTIONAL RESONANCE TO THE VISUALS

It's possible that each color family has a different emotional resonance for you. They may bring up memories, both happy and sad.

Do you have favorite colors? Take some time to explore why some colors are your favorite.

Some colors might make you feel better or worse than others. That's okay. You can choose to use

16

whatever colors you prefer and leave others completely unused. No one said all the tools in the box must be used. This is another form of freedom.

If the feelings you get from some colors aren't too overwhelming, at some point you might want to explore the memories that come up for you. Start with the closest thought, and as you continue to color in the image in front of you, mentally trace the thoughts back to the root.

This process can take as long or be as fast as you like. You don't need answers by the time you complete coloring the current page, nor do you need them by the end of the book. There are always other coloring books and new sets of pencils and pens. There is time.

THE SENSE OF SIGHT AND MEMORY

It's possible that each color family resonates inside you with a different set of feelings. They may bring up memories, which you might perceive as either light or dark, or maybe even mixed.

Tracing happy feelings back to their inception might unveil a part of you which you had forgotten and would be happy to reintegrate into your life.

Tracing sad or angry feelings backward might help you release those feelings all together. Forgiving others can transform your relationships and how you fit into the world. Forgiving yourself can transform your relationship with various aspects of self and unlock the best you—the one who you know exists deep inside.

CHILDHOOD MEMORIES

Coloring is something many of us did when we were young. The act of coloring now, as an adult, can spark memories that have long lain dormant.

How you perceive the memories or the labels that you give them, like happy or sad, do not mean they are either good or bad. They are just memories, which are colored by time and viewed through the lens of the present. Your memories might not even be "real" in the strictest sense of that word.

Maybe we do not remember all of the facts of what happened correctly.

Sometimes we fill in the foggy parts of a memory with stuff that never actually happened.

Whatever comes up for you, continue the act of coloring.

In this way, we can get in touch with the child within, and rekindle a relationship with the YOU from so many years ago. The one who played with abandon and reveled in the wild fancies of imagination. This inner child will reveal to you deep dreams long forgotten and areas where you could use some self-nurturing.

MEMORIES—STORY VERSUS FACT

The facts of what happened in the past sometimes get interwoven with our emotional responses to those "facts". We often make up a meaning about ourselves or about others.

An example: I remember a time in junior high school where I was running for vice president of the student body. I remember being embarrassed when I delivered a poorly prepared skit in front of all the students gathered in the cafeteria. Those are the facts. I made a meaning about who I am at the core from that experience which was "I am no good at speaking in front of large audiences." That meaning became a part of my identity, but it is not the truth. That meaning I made is only my interpretation of the facts, created by me as a child to help protect me from future embarrassment.

Pause your coloring for a moment, and ask yourself, "Have I colored out of the lines? Have I messed up somewhere on this page?" Chances are, the thought had already arisen in your awareness before you read this.

This type of question happens to us all in so many forms throughout a given day. It seems reasonable enough. But if we are honest, it is also a form of judgement or self-criticism. Error is implicit in asking such a question. And this is like my personal example. There are the facts of what happened—we colored outside the lines—and there is the meaning we place over the facts like a blanket thrown over a bed.

In your past, did someone—maybe someone in your family—ever tell you what it meant about you when you colored outside the lines?

Try it. Go ahead, make a mistake. Color outside the lines right now. Screw it up. Make a person's face striped magenta and neon green. What's the worst that can happen? You might even feel liberated from some self-imposed boundaries.

Chapter 3

Hearing and Listening

LISTENING WITH PURPOSE

Focus on the rhythmic sound of the tip of the pen or pencil as it goes back and forth across the paper.

Ask yourself, "Is it different if I press harder or softer?"

"Does the cap of my pen make a sound when I take if off? What about when I snap it back on?"

If you are feeling heavy emotions, like sadness or panic, try focusing on these simple sounds of your coloring activity. Chances are it will help reduce external distractions and focus on the present moment.

ANOTHER LAYER OF SOUND

What does a pencil sound like when it is being sharpened? Does it key you in to the fact that the pencil and paper are made of real wood? It's a material that comes from nature. This activity connects you to the greater world around you.

Think about where it came from. Imagine a forest. What kind of forest? There are different forests depending on what part of the world you imagine. Some forests drop their leaves in winter. Others are evergreen, like the pines of climes close to the North and South poles or high in the mountains. Then there are bamboo forests and rainforests. Maybe you can envision others.

The (sustainably grown) tree which gave life to this product of personal expression in your hand or at your fingertips started as a seed. It progressed from sprout to sapling to a small tree vying for sunlight. That you hold a piece of it in your hand is miraculous. It lives on in the patterns you color and the little bit of calm and serenity you are creating in this moment.

THE SOUNDS OF VICTORY

How often do we ever notice the pages of a book or magazine turning? Each ruffle of paper and flipping motion is a little victory for your wellbeing. Why not make a ritual of it?

Hear the page as if flips over to reveal the next image. Appreciate the coloring you just finished and take in the new image before you. Pump your fist in the air. Do a little dance. Say, "Victory!" out loud. Maybe not a full shout, depending on where you are, but at least whisper it and pat yourself on the back. Take notice and celebrate that you took the time to nurture yourself. Self-acknowledgement is powerful. You deserve it.

SURROUND SOUND

When you color, you move your body. That means wherever you are, your body and whatever it is in contact with could be making noise.

Are your shoes scuffling the floor? Or is your knee bobbing up and down with pent-up energy?

Is the chair or couch creaking? Do your clothes swish or rub? The sounds might be subtle.

These sounds aren't anything to dwell on either. Just make note that you heard it and then let the thought pass. Other items of awareness are always arising. There is never a shortage. They come unbidden and float away and shift in form like puffy spring clouds.

FAR OUT SOUNDS

Push your awareness out further. Are there birds outside chirping? Is there an air conditioner or heater humming?

Are there people talking? If so, are they close by or far away? The quality of their voices can vary with distance.

Sometimes you might perceive an echo, other times their murmuring will be so soft that none of their words will be distinct.

Other times their voices will be so clear you could easily believe they were being amplified by a microphone and speakers.

Note the varying nature and form of the sounds. And then let them mix together and fade into the background as you again focus on your coloring.

SOUNDS FURTHER AFIELD

Push your awareness out further still.

With the direction and speed of winds, sounds will carry in the strangest of ways. Every day is different, even if you color in the same exact spot and in the same comfortable chair day after day.

Are there cars and trucks or a train out there? Can you hear individual engines revving nearby, then trailing off as they drive away from you?

There might be road hum from lots of traffic if you are near a big highway or bridge. See how far out you can hear, and let your being expand with that awareness.

A WIDE, WONDERFUL WORLD OF SOUNDS

Push your awareness out as far as you can, past the immediate sounds, and past any people nearby.

Can you hear the weather?

What about rain falling? Is it light drizzle or a downpour? How can you tell? What are the signs you notice today?

There could be leaves rustling in the wind along the ground. It might be different depending on the surface over which they roll. Grass. Rocks. Blacktop. Concrete.

Or wind could be whipping through the branches of trees.

There is a world of wonder living within the small differences denoted by your awareness in the present moment.

Chapter 4

Touch

THE WORLD THROUGH FINGERTIPS

Take the pencil or pen in your hand. Close your eyes and feel the contours.

Is it smooth? Does it have ridges?

What about the weight? Is it balanced or does one end feel heavier than the other?

Would you describe it as soft or hard?

How about cool or warm?

Does the tip feel different than the main part of the pen or pencil? No peeking... Can you tell a difference in material solely with your hands?

Whatever you feel or sense, it is what is, and nothing more. No right and no wrong.

CONNECTION TO THE PHYSICAL WORLD

Can you feel the paper through the pen or pencil tip and up into your hands? You might find that some paper is silky smooth, while other paper types have a texture which provides a little resistance as you color.

Is there difference between how the cover of your book feels and the pages inside feel? Is the cover glossy or matte?

Can you sense the subtle texture of the pages with your fingertips? Maybe the lines of ink which make up the image before you color feel different than the clean, empty spaces in the margins.

IN THE PRESENT YOU CAN TOUCH THE PAST OR FUTURE

Your coloring book might be a new acquaintance or an old, trusted friend. Each one will have a different character in your hands.

Edges may be frayed.

New pages and spines might be rigid. Do you have to press back the cover to get the image to lay flat?

Books which have seen more of your attention might easily fall open to the latest page which has your attention.

By taking in subtle details in the present moment you can glimpse the past or future. How miraculous is that?

Chapter 5

The Sense of Smell

GROUNDING SCENTS

The smell of a new book is full of promise.

Breathe in deeply through your nose. It's a subtle mixture of paper and ink.

Flip through the pages with the book right in front of your nose. Pick a few adjectives that describe the sensation.

Or maybe this coloring book has been with you for some time. Were you at a cafe the last time you colored? The scent of roasted coffee beans, toasted tea, and brewed goodness might be infused into your book.

In sensing what is in front of you now, you naturally let go of thoughts and stories, worries and anxieties.

SNIFFING, NOT HUFFING

The smell of each book is a little bit different.

Your pencils might have their own, woody aroma. And then there's the box in which the pencils or pens came. Or the case you transferred them into.

If you use gel pens, are they devoid of smell?

Does the ink have a scent?

But don't sniff too long… if they are strong, you might get a little lightheaded, and we don't want that! We are practicing in our own simple way the powerful technique of mindfulness, not forgetfulness.

Chapter 6

The Sense of Taste

DO COLORS HAVE A FLAVOR?

This one is a little strange, but bear with me...

Don't lick your pen or pencil and certainly don't chomp down. Likely they are non-toxic and as green as can be, but they aren't edible.

But maybe you are drinking some tea, coffee, water, or something else.

Water has a taste. Most people don't notice it. Swish it in your mouth and see if you can detect something.

Maybe you have a snack. Salty, sweet, crunchy, sour, bitter, smooth, rough?

Revel in the subtle flavors as your continue to color away.

Part 3

Coloring and Mindfulness

Chapter 7

The Practice of Noting

MENTAL STICK PINS

Oftentimes you will find thoughts swimming into your mind from nowhere. They do that. That's the nature of how our minds work. Thoughts come unbidden.

You might not even realize it for a while. You've gone down the rabbit of hole of thought, leading from a thought to yet another thought.

Once you recognize that the thoughts have taken control, you can use a simple technique that dissolves the power and grip of those thoughts. It's called *Noting*.

You simply note or say to yourself (either out loud or in your mind), "thinking". We simply give our current state of being a one word label. It's like you are taking a stick pin and calling out the nature of your experience. You are tagging a label onto it.

This helps you let go of either thinking of past events or how you might deal with things in the future. Noting puts a pin in the thought and brings you back to the present moment.

NOTING, A SECOND DIMENSION

There is another dimension to the technique of Noting. We can have a chicken and egg dilemma. Sometimes thoughts give rise to feelings. Other times we feel an emotion, which then brings up our thinking to figure out why we feel that way. Sometimes we think of ways to avoid a feeling, in the case of "bad" emotions, or reinforce the feeling, in the case of "good" emotions.

So, if you catch yourself floating away from the present moment on a current of emotion, simply noting or saying to yourself the single word "feeling" will help you see it for what it is. The feeling is not you. It arises within the conscious mind, but it just as easily can float away.

NOTING IN 3D

The third dimension of Noting is calling out sensation. These are the physical manifestations of having a body. Maybe your foot itches. Or your back is tight. Or you feel a roll of fat at your waistline.

These sensations often kick off thoughts and feelings. So, wherever you become conscious in the stream of thought, feeling, and sensation, just call it out with gentleness. There is no need for judgement or analysis.

And, of course you might wonder if the act of noting is itself thinking. The answer is yes, if we want to be logically accurate, but the pins you place with noting are single slivers of time that have no hold on your experience of the now. There's no need to recursively note that you are noting. That would be counterproductive.

In noting the noting, you just might conclude how absurd the whole thing is. Give in to that. Laugh out loud. Let go of the control. The emptiness that follows is like a flower's nectar to a butterfly. A moment of sweetness.

NOTING SIMPLIFIED

If you like, sensation can be further broken down into the five senses: hearing, touching, smelling, seeing, tasting. But now you have eight total words to keep track of. We want to simplify this process of being in the present moment, this experience of being mindful.

If you really want to, go for it with this additional layer of noting. Just know that the idea is to make this as easy as possible. We are not taking a test. This isn't a job interview where right and wrong answers might be judged. There really is no way to fail, as long as you keep breathing and continue giving the technique a try.

Chapter 8

Visualization

A WINNING VISUALIZATION

There are many ways to incorporate visualization in our day-to-day lives.

Perhaps the best-known area of application of visualization in western culture is in competitive sports. A sprinter might visualize a hundred-meter dash to see in her mind's eye the perfect race. She could imagine how snug her clothes feel and the temperature of the air. She might imagine the angle of the sun or the sound of her feet settling into the starting blocks. Then there's the crack of the gun and the motion of coiled tension being released. She imagines each stride, each breath, and each pump of her arms.

And, of course there's the first-place finish, and maybe even a world record up on the digital board. The crowd roars as she takes her victory lap, her country's flag waving high over her head.

The technique can be used anywhere, anytime, for any purpose: right before a race or sitting in a dentist's waiting room.

VISUALIZATION TRANSFORMS THE FUTURE

Visualization can be practiced by anyone, and is particularly powerful for those of us who come from dysfunctional backgrounds or who have endured trauma.

If we find ourselves chronically reacting to specific, stressful situations, we can use visualization to see ourselves calmly weathering what once made us angry, afraid, panicked, or paralyzed.

Visualization gives us a safe way to run through a future event and refine the outcome, again and again, until we start to expect good things happening to us.

Try it right now with your coloring. See in your mind what the finished product will look like. Imagine how you will feel as you finish. The stakes are low on this one, so why not close your eyes for a minute and visualize the act of coloring the next page?

Chapter 9

Attending to the Breath

BUT I ALREADY KNOW HOW TO BREATHE

Each time you select a new color, take a moment to take in a slow, deep breath. As you let out the breath slowly, view the page you are working on.

Are you focusing on a singular spot on the page? Perhaps the last spot you colored?

Take in another breath, deep in your belly, a little more air than the last time. Hold your breath in. Now try to take in the whole page with your awareness, without fixating on any one point. Then let the breath out.

Your body absorbed all the oxygen from that big, replenishing breath. Now, try to maintain breath awareness as you color again. Sometimes you might find that as you concentrate, your breath becomes shallow. When you notice this, just simply pause and take in another long lungful of replenishing air.

BREATHING AWARENESS PRACTICE

Let's try an awareness practice to help anchor you to the present moment. In contrast to exercises that work on healthful breathing techniques, we will simply attend to the breath.

Whether it is shallow or deep, long or short, smooth, rough, coarse or defined, we just notice how it is without the need to change it in any way.

Breathing in gives way to breathing out, and on and on it goes. In simply attending to the breath, we begin to notice the impermanence of any current state of being.

Thoughts come unbidden, and on their backs, we sometimes experience feelings. Some pleasant. Some discomforting. Meditative practice helps us to not cling to things. And the faster we let things pass, as all things do anyway, we begin to experience more and more liberation from our thoughts and feelings.

44

HOW MANY BREATHS?

"How many breaths are enough?" If we are talking about our lifetimes, I would have to say, "All of them!" But for our purposes of being aware of the present moment, let's say ten is enough.

It is sometimes helpful to have an anchor when practicing awareness of our bodies in the present moment.

A simple way to settle us into awareness is to count our breaths. Count one in your mind as you inhale as you normally would. There is no need to force deeper breathing. Count two as you exhale. Then three on the next inhale, and so on. When you reach ten, you can start over again at one on the next breath.

See if you can attend to a single inhale or exhale, keeping your awareness focused solely on the continuous line of the expanding or contracting breath.

You can do this exercise to remove anxiety or worry from any physical or creative task you are doing. Try it while doodling with your pens or pencils, or while filling in the designs in your favorite coloring book.

BREATHING IN THE BOX

Boxed breathing is a simple technique to try any time you feel stressed or anxious. This technique, also referred to as four-square breathing, emphasizes control through four counts of four, and it allows your body to make full use of the air you breathe. Calm your nerves and relieve stress by helping to reset the autonomic nervous system.

Step 1: Sit up straight and rest your hands on your lap. We want your posture aligned and your body at ease.

Step 2: Ideally you want to be in a quiet space with your eyes closed where the telephone, smart device, or people won't bother you for at least four minutes. That said, the privacy isn't an imperative. You can still get benefits with your eyes open on a packed subway or a bustling coffee shop.

Step 3: Breathe in through your nose and slowly count to four as you inhale, filling your lungs. Concentrate on you belly and recognize that it also expands as you inhale deeply. Now hold your breath for four seconds.

Step 4: Slowly exhale through your mouth to a count of four. Then hold the exhale for another four count. Repeat for a few minutes.

If you are a deep breather, your four count might be a lot longer than four seconds. That's perfectly fine, too.

If this technique is good enough to calm the nerves of Navy Seals on covert missions, it's good enough for the stresses of daily modern life.

BOXED BREATHING—PART 2

In through the nose for a four count, hold for four. Out through the mouth for four, and hold the exhale for four to finish. Repeat tracing the box. With each iteration, allow the air to fill your belly more deeply.

One of the goals of four-square breathing is to realign the respiratory system. The body falls into the shallow breathing patterns of the flight or fight response when under stress, both physical and emotional. Research shows that in addition to alleviating stress, controlled breathing can treat insomnia, anxiety, depression and response to pain.

If you find that you continue dwelling on specific thoughts, try saying a mantra in your head. Repeat a calming sound as you breathe. The yoga "ohm" isn't just for New-Agey spiritualism. When said out loud, it's a tried-and-true way to relax the jaw and face muscles.

As you continue with the exercise, your concentration will begin to narrow, and troublesome thoughts and feelings will lose their weight and melt away.

Chapter 10

Transcendental Meditation

YOUR PERSONAL MANTRA

Counting each breath in and out up to 10 and starting over might not be so great if you have obsessive tendencies. It can become like trying to count sheep up to 1017 when trying to fall asleep. It's possible that the numbers mean something to you that ramps your anxiety. Who knows, maybe you have an uncomfortable experience with rating things, 1 to 10 from "not so hot" to "awesome". If so, maybe that's something to explore at some later date.

For now, let's try a variation of attending to something regular and physical. It's time to pick your very own Personal Mantra. It is simply a combination of sounds which mean nothing in your native language. Your mantra is yours alone, and it gives you a sensation that is void of meaning to focus on.

Synching your personal mantra to your breath can give you a deep sense of calm. Vowel sounds like "ah", "oo", "oh" help ground you in your breath. You can say it out loud, or say it inside your head as you breathe. It works either way.

I know that when I first started this exercise I had a lot of fun with it. I got to play with the little kid in me. I tried all kinds of mantras. I explored how they made me feel, both physically and emotionally. Some sounds made my lips vibrate so much they tickled. I found different sounds got me in touch with different parts of my body. The chest for some. My nasal passages for others. Even my shoulders and neck.

Think of this as a game where you don't have to keep track of the score. Explore the boundaries of what seems right or proper to you. Have fun testing out the possibilities. Finding your Personal Mantra is about learning to let go.

If the exercise feels super serious, try smiling and making the most ridiculous laughing sounds you can. That's a sure-fire way to loosen the shackles of needing to maintain your illusion of control.

Chapter 11

A Rainbow of Tools for Happiness

You have learned and practiced a bunch of amazing tools that have begun to unlock some powerful mysteries of mindfulness and awareness.

We have either introduced you to totally new techniques or helped you reinforce skills you already practice. These include...

- Mindful breathing

- Noting thoughts, feelings, and sensations as they arise

- Visualization

- Settling into the present moment through sense awareness, and

- Expanding and contracting your mental focus

And you have not only strengthened your emotional fortitude and eased your mind, you have also anchored these lessons into your physical world, through the act of coloring in a meditative manner.

Your mind and emotional responses are forever linked to your body.

Tony Robbins, a master change agent who has helped millions of people worldwide transform themselves, says that the quickest way to change what you are feeling is to change your physical state.

You have practiced that by being mindful of...

> - *Your posture when you color*
>
> - *How the tools you use look and feel and sound*
>
> - *Your breathing patterns*

Who knew that something as fun and relaxing as coloring could be such a powerful tool for healing and personal development?

About the Author

DIGITAL STORYTELLER

Writer ~ Narrator ~ Entrepreneur

Once, I was a scientist—not the soft stuff, but physics. Then one day—while carbon-dating the Shroud of Turin, or was it designing microprocessors for Apple?—I chucked it all to become a storyteller. I studied filmmaking in Prague and acting in NYC.

I've played Jesus, Robert Kennedy and LBJ in the same production, and even a WWII Nazi-Vampire.

CUBIK, the Singapore-set Techno-thriller film I co-wrote & directed, won the Grand Remi Prize at WorldFest—the same as Spielberg's first award.

These days, I focus on writing novels, producing audiobooks and podcasts, and teaching simple ways to generate lasting habits for happiness.

Visit **jasonbrenizer.com** to learn more...

About Unlock My ZEN

You can learn more about our range of coloring books for adults and other resources that help you wash away stress and anxiety at...

UnlockMyZEN.com

Not only will you discover inspiring images to color, you will also receive gentle lessons in gratitude, explorations into the teachers of past wisdom, insights on self-healing, and habits for happiness.

You can also engage with us at the *Unlock My ZEN* Facebook page, *UMZ* Instagram account, or the *Adult Coloring Book Society* Facebook page.

Please upload a picture of your latest coloring masterpiece to any of our social sites to share it with our community. We love to see you making progress on your journey toward fulfillment, serenity, and true happiness.

We often hold giveaway contests and offer bonuses for all of you out there taking your happiness into your own hands and using our tools to help eradicate stress, worry, and anxiety.

Let's color it all away together to develop your best self!

www.ingramcontent.com/pod-product-compliance
Lightning Source LLC
Chambersburg PA
CBHW060040040426
42331CB00032B/1903